A Child's Book of
Miracles & Wonders

Illustrated by
Trace Moroney

Retold by
Mildred A. Tuck

**CANDLE
BOOKS**

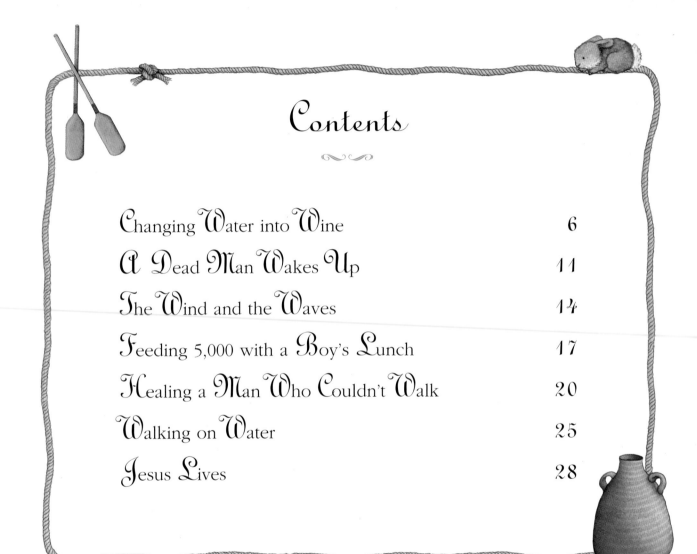

Contents

Introduction

While he was on earth, Jesus performed many miracles to help and heal people. A miracle is something only God can do—something that can't be explained by ordinary means. Miracles show us how powerful God is, how much he loves us, and how he cares about what happens to us.

Jesus' friends wrote about his miracles in the Bible. This book retells seven of these very special events. You will read how Jesus raised people from the dead, made the sick well, fed a huge crowd with just a young boy's lunch, and much more.

You will also see why Jesus did these wonderful things—to show everyone that he was the Son of God.

Changing Water into Wine

John 2:1–11

〰

Jesus and his friends went to a wedding. His mother, Mary, was there also. It was a wonderful party and everyone was having a great time. Then Mary overheard some of the servants talking.

"We've run out of wine," said one. "What should we do?" The other just shrugged his shoulders. "I don't know. The family will be very embarrassed if the guests have no wine to drink." Quickly, Mary ran to tell Jesus.

"But mother," Jesus answered, "why are you saying this to me? It's not time for me to show people who I am yet." But Mary called the servants over and said, "Do whatever my son tells you."

〰 6 〰

Jesus pointed to six large jars nearby. "Fill those with water," he told the servants. When they had finished, Jesus said, "Now pour some out and take it to the master of the banquet." The servants did as they were instructed, then stepped aside to watch.

The master of the banquet took a sip from the cup. He looked puzzled, but drank again, this time until the cup was empty. Then he called over to the bridegroom. "People generally serve the good wine first," he said. "But you have saved the very best for last!"

This was the first miracle Jesus performed. And when his friends saw it, they knew that he was truly the Son of God.

☀ Heavenly Father, teach me to follow Jesus' example, and to remember how it pleases you. Amen.

A Dead Man Wakes Up

John 11:1–45

There were two sisters, Mary and Martha, who had a brother named Lazarus. They were all good friends with Jesus, and he loved them very much. While Jesus was visiting another city, the sisters sent a message for him to come right away because Lazarus was sick.

Four days later, Jesus finally arrived at Mary and Martha's house. But by then, Lazarus was dead. Martha was very upset.

Then Jesus said, "Your brother will live again for I am the resurrection and the life. Anyone who believes in me will have life even though he dies. And anyone who lives and believes in me will never die. Martha, do you believe this?"

Martha nodded her head and said, "Yes, Lord, I have always believed that you are the Son of God." Then Martha went to tell Mary that Jesus had arrived. Mary got up quickly and ran to meet Jesus.

She fell down at his feet and said, "Lord, if you had been here, my brother would still be alive."

When Jesus saw Mary crying, he also began to cry.

Then, Mary and Martha took Jesus to the cave where Lazarus had been buried. When they arrived, Jesus said, "Take away the stone." After the rock was moved, Jesus called out in a loud voice, "Lazarus, come out!"

The people waited and watched. From the darkness of the cave, Lazarus came out. He was alive! His hands, feet, and face were wrapped with pieces of cloth. Jesus told his friends to help unwrap Lazarus and let him go. Many believed in Jesus after they saw him perform this wondrous miracle.

☀ Dear God, thank you for raising Lazarus from the dead. Help me to remember how great you are. Amen.

The Wind and the Waves

Matthew 8:23–27

Jesus was tired. After a long day of teaching, he got into a boat with his friends to go across the lake, and fell asleep.

Suddenly, dark clouds burst open and rain came pouring down. The winds blew hard and the waves slammed against the boat.

Jesus' friends were terrified. They looked at Jesus. He was still sleeping. "Teacher! Teacher!" they shouted. "Help us, please. We are going to drown!" Jesus heard their cries and woke up.

"Why are you so afraid?" he asked them. "Don't you trust me to protect you?" Then Jesus got up and commanded the wind and the waves to be still. At once, the wind stopped and the sea became calm. The men looked at each other in amazement. "What kind of man is this?" they said. "Even the wind and the sea obey him!"

Dear Jesus, thank you that you are in control of everything. Amen.

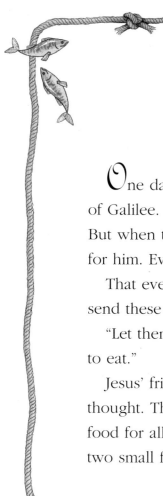

Feeding 5,000 with a Boy's Lunch

Matthew 14:13–21

One day, Jesus took a boat to a peaceful place along the shores of Galilee. He wanted to spend some time away from the crowds. But when the boat reached shore, thousands of people were waiting for him. Even though Jesus was tired, he continued to heal them.

That evening, Jesus' friends came to him and said, "You must send these people away so they can get food for themselves."

"Let them stay," Jesus answered. "And *you* give them something to eat."

Jesus' friends looked at one another. *That's impossible,* they thought. Then they said, "But where are we going to get enough food for all these people? We only have five loaves of bread and two small fish from a young boy who gave us his lunch."

"Bring what you have to me," Jesus said. Then he told the crowd to sit on the grass. Jesus took the loaves and fish, looked up to heaven, and asked God's blessing on the food. He broke the bread and fish into smaller pieces, then gave them to his friends to hand out to the hungry people.

As they did this, they were astonished to see there was plenty of food. And, when everyone was full, there were 12 baskets of food left over!

☀ Dear Lord, help me to remember that nothing is too hard or impossible for you to do. Thank you for always giving me everything I need. Amen.

Healing a Man Who Couldn't Walk

Mark 2:1–12

large crowd gathered in a house to hear Jesus. The room was completely full and even more people stood outside. Just then, four men approached. They were bringing their friend, who could not walk, to Jesus to be healed. First, they tried to get through the crowd. Then, when they couldn't, they climbed up on the roof, cut out a hole, and lowered their friend into the room on a mat.

The people moved aside as the mat dropped down in front of Jesus. Jesus saw all that these men had done, and knew they really believed in him. So he took the paralyzed man's hand and said, "Your sins are forgiven."

The teachers and priests grumbled at this. *"Who does he think he is?"* they said to themselves. *"Only God can forgive sins."* But Jesus knew what they were thinking. So he said to them, "I could tell this man 'Your sins are forgiven,' or 'Take your mat, get up, and walk.' But I will prove to you, that as God's Son, I have the right to forgive sins." Then Jesus turned to the man and said, "Stand up, young man, and carry your bed home."

The man put his feet on the floor and stood. He thanked Jesus, picked up his bed, and walked out of the house. All the people who saw this were amazed and praised God.

☀ Dear Jesus, Thank you that you not only have the power to heal, but also to forgive sins. Amen.

Walking on Water

Matthew 14:22–33

~∞~

Jesus decided to go to the mountainside to pray by himself. He told his friends to take a boat across to the other side and he would meet them later. But when they had reached the centre of the lake, the wind began to blow hard and the waves made the small boat rock back and forth. The men were afraid.

But Jesus knew that his friends needed help. So he went out to them by walking on top of the water. At first, the men couldn't tell that it was Jesus. They thought he was a ghost and cried out in fear.

"Do not be afraid," Jesus called to them. "It's me."

"If it's you, Lord," Peter shouted back, "then let me walk out to you on the water."

"Come then," Jesus answered.

Peter got out of the boat and took a few steps. *I'm really walking on water,* he thought. Then he looked away from Jesus, down to the wind and waves, and got frightened. Right away, he began to sink. "Lord, please save me!" he shouted.

Jesus reached out and caught his hand. "Why did you doubt?" Jesus asked him.

As soon as they climbed back into the boat, the storm stopped and the water was calm. Peter and the other men were amazed at the things they had just seen.

☀ Dear Jesus, thank you that you are stronger than anything I am afraid of. Help me remember to trust you the next time I get scared. Amen.

Jesus Lives

John 20:1–18

❧❧❧

Jesus was put on a cross to die because his enemies didn't believe he was the Son of God. After he had died, his friends wrapped his body in linen, and put him inside a tomb. A big stone was rolled in front of the opening.

Three days later, Mary Magdalene went to the place they put Jesus and was amazed to find the huge rock had been moved away. So she ran to tell Jesus' friends what had happened. When Peter and John returned to the tomb, they found the wrappings Jesus was buried in folded neatly on the ground. They saw this and knew what Jesus said was true. He had risen from the dead!

Then Jesus' friends went back home. But Mary stayed outside the tomb, crying. Just then, she heard a voice say, "Why are you crying?" When she looked up, she saw two angels sitting inside the cave.

"They have taken away my Lord, and I don't know where they have put him," she answered. Then Mary noticed someone standing behind her. She thought he might be the gardener. "Sir," she asked, "Did you see who took the body from this cave?"

"Mary!" the man said. Mary knew that voice. She could not believe her eyes. It was Jesus! "Teacher!" she cried out. "You're alive!"

"Yes, I'm going to heaven to be with my father," Jesus said. "Go now, and tell everyone that you have seen me."

☀ Heavenly Father, you are the source of all miracles and wonders. Thank you for raising Jesus from the dead and promising that I can join him and you one day in heaven. Amen.